Sarah's Tap Shoes

Adapted by Benjamin Hulme-Cross

Sarah gets tap shoes.

Can Sarah's shoes tap here?
No they can not.

Can Sarah's shoes tap here?

4

No they can not.

Can Sarah's shoes tap here?

No they can not.

Can Sarah's shoes tap here?
Yes they can!